# SO MUCH SYNTH

ALSO BY BRENDA SHAUGHNESSY

*Our Andromeda*
*Human Dark with Sugar*
*Interior with Sudden Joy*

# BRENDA SHAUGHNESSY
# SO MUCH SYNTH

COPPER CANYON PRESS

PORT TOWNSEND, WASHINGTON

Cover art: Emma Nicholson, detail of Island Sunset faux fur

Copper Canyon Press is in residence at Fort Worden State Park in Port Townsend, Washington, under the auspices of Centrum. Centrum is a gathering place for artists and creative thinkers from around the world, students of all ages and backgrounds, and audiences seeking extraordinary cultural enrichment.

LIBRARY OF CONGRESS CATALOGING-IN-PUBLICATION DATA

Names: Shaughnessy, Brenda, 1970– author.
Title: So much synth / Brenda Shaughnessy.
Description: Port Townsend, Washington : Copper Canyon Press, [2016]
Identifiers: LCCN 2015042109 | ISBN 9781556594878 (hardcover)
Subjects: | BISAC: POETRY / American / Asian American.
Classification: LCC PS3569.H353 A6 2016 | DDC 811/.54—dc23
LC record available at http://lccn.loc.gov/2015042109

98765432 FIRST PRINTING

COPPER CANYON PRESS
Post Office Box 271
Port Townsend, Washington 98368
www.coppercanyonpress.org

# CONTENTS

## IV. SECRETS SEE ME COMING

# SO MUCH SYNTH

## I Have a Time Machine

But unfortunately it can only travel into the future
at a rate of one second per second,

which seems slow to the physicists and to the grant
committees and even to me.

But I manage to get there, time after time, to the next
moment and to the next.

Thing is, I can't turn it off. I keep zipping ahead—
well not *zipping*—And if I try

to get out of this time machine, open the latch,
I'll fall into space, unconscious,

then desiccated! And I'm pretty sure I'm afraid of that.
So I stay inside.

There's a window, though. It shows the past.
It's like a television or fish tank.

But it's never live; it's always over. The fish swim
in backward circles.

Sometimes it's like a rearview mirror, another chance
to see what I'm leaving behind,

and sometimes like blackout, all that time
wasted sleeping.

Myself age eight, whole head burnt with embarrassment
at having lost a library book.

Myself lurking in a candled corner expecting
to be found charming.

Me holding a rose though I want to put it down
so I can smoke.

Me exploding at my mother who explodes at me
because the explosion

of some dark star all the way back struck hard
at mother's mother's mother.

I turn away from the window, anticipating a blow.
I thought I'd find myself

an old woman by now, traveling so light in time.
But I haven't gotten far at all.

Strange not to be able to pick up the pace as I'd like;
the past is so horribly fast.

# I. EDGEHOLE

## McQueen Is Dead. Long Live McQueen

There were seven colors of mourning,
one was lilac. That kind of blossom

always has its crowd, fanned out, surrounded
by crushing likeness, smell of itself.

> Fabric has to breathe,
> at least 2 percent, like skin.

> A little milkfat, elastin
> even in the gravest print.

Not knowing how to grieve can poison
like a directionless dart. And although fabric

> has been known to swirl
> and clasp, be clasped—

> without mother
> there's only art.

To hug the body: a swath, anathema,
magical, '70s lace and spacedust,

> all too far gone

to truly love. But to twist it, to learn
to hate-want. To sway, tear, burrow,

> be borrowed,
> everybody's animal.

To float like water seeking its own,
stampede like buffalo, seeking its hide.

Face painted on torso on horsehair
on chesty silk it's a deathmask

> for the stigmata slashes
> of the model's body.

※    ※

I don't think I understand what studying is.
I listen, I read, I remember, I absorb.

I let myself be moved and changed.
Is that "studying?"

> Never five-fingered,
> you never use them all,
>
> gloves will be like hooves,
> split-footed hand-stitched.

When concept perceived—a womanly gist, let's say,
or a curve of mind—is more than itself (surpassing,

all maw), I make it part of me. I take it in,
drink a corrosive. I let it overtake me,

> change everything it can,
> lip to tip to rim.

My eyes just drink the fabric that covers
each surface of this world.

> Suck up the plastic
> through a polished straw.

Everything's inspiration: trees reflected
in windows on buildings, distorted buses,

                    endless frames, all too glass,
                    so much lens, textures so tall,

and once you start to see things this way,
vision's a performance, shocking

and true after all these centuries,
a Shakespearean volta, like nectar

                    is poison to the occasional
                    queen bee.

Everything actually is blurred,
not just how you see.

Glasses and shoes are solutions
to problems that are real problems,

                    that of blurred world,
                    that of touching the ground.

A glass corset for the heart
to see out its chest. For without

glasses, the eye better sees
the wind, by feeling it and closing

                    against its grains,
                    its grasses.

For without shoes, my feet become
shoes. When I am really feeling,

I get very tired, I fall asleep
for the seventeenth time

                    on the unfinished skirt
                    of glass eyes and lemon

zest hemmed first,
grown last.

I experience the world as infinite
invertedness: no wholes broken,

just potential fragments straining, skull-like,
at the seams. Anything could give.

But no, just takes
and takes and takes.

⚹    ⚹

I've been trying to write the words,
"I cried. Cried really

and wetly, and for good." Old-fashioned
writing with intense excitement:

the spell of quill
and ink spill, quelled.

What is beautiful, what is terrifying,
what is absurd in me?

Every possibility that colors
are believable, various—

not that mirage
I thought I'd seen—

and can be held apart as unreal,
too exterior, distinct from each

other wildly as sparks to seaweed
or flower to meteor.

It collapsed, can't draw it,
can't cut it out of itself.

There is no color but what's already
inside the eye, no power

or invention or new way to wake up
in the morning

                    outside the seeing
                    mechanism,

our own orbs. Yet I can't see myself.
I can never see you again.

I can only see from inside my skull
and when I look down

                    I close everything
                    not just my eyes.

I wrap my own tender nether flesh
in calfskin leather so buttery,

                    melted back
                    together

like so: a newborn softened
in its own mother's milk.


            ✖       ✖


I awoke in a panic (no ma no ma) to the smallest day yet.
I dreamed I already

dreamed all the dreams I'd get.
This morning I dressed

in my last dress's
last dress,

fit only for a genteel gothic
murder, covered up well—airtight,

would only fit the stabbed one,
after bloodlet.

Then, like a glove.

Who wears it and where?
I will, from the bed to the chair.

Headrest, clotheshorse.
Designer and model: mutually orbiting

the best metaphor for bodiless idea.
Amorphous, amorous, amoral,

immortal. Red is dead,
said blue, to you too?

Hindquarter-gauze with silver faceclamp
and sickened ears pulled,

unskulled.

Broken backpiece. Shadow sensible
by other than sight. To smell a shadow.

To strike it. To trace it later,
to measure a body by its line.

Light's so quiet.

You'd think its cuttings, its edge-hole,
those mousy children, would squeak

at least a bit. They run like a stocking
down the leg of the mind.

                   Why not quieter then?

There is no body without life.
There is no mind without body.

                   There is no without.

## Last Sleep, Best Sleep

Life, this charade of not-death.
Amnesiac of our nights together,

overheard talking in some other voice.
The great fruits of my failure:

silk milk pills with little bitter pits.
Who talks like that? Says we are

ever-locked, leaving everything
petaled and veined the way nature

pretended. Synthesized within
an inch of its life. Oh the many faces

of facelessness, breathing in the dark—
as if we could shape softness itself,

mold it around us like yams mashed
against a trough by a snuffling snout.

Our own. There's no way out. Born
to such extra, we are born to lose.

No hairy fingers tapering to threads,
grasping for some lost last use.

Once we were hungry on earth,
soon buried like root vegetables—

to starve the soil as beets do,
growing in our graves.

But now we must remember
our way back to face-to-face,

to eye to eye and hand in hand,
and lock and step and key in hole.

Remembering how not to fall asleep,
we become so desperately drowsy,

and all cells strain to slow to a stop.
All desire to choose otherwise quiets.

No, no one can say we didn't suffer,
that we weren't swallowed whole.

## Living Will

If I make a decision now, but die
before enacting it, does my last decision stay
in limbo, alive without a body?

Or does it die with me, becoming no decision,
undoing my last choice on this earth as if
I had already died before I died?

And what if my last decision was: I would like to die.
Does that make a point or abandon it, my life
a question with no mark, answered before asked?

And if so, and I was already, in this way, dead
before I made my last decision,
how long was I dead before that?

Wanting to die, deciding to die or not, already lost
and gone, not only irrelevant in the last moment
but having diminished all along,

not knowing when the diminishment began.
Perhaps it never began; I was always
lessening, losing, disappearing,

from my first breath, imperceptibly at first.
Then, not at but near the end: canceled in totality.
It would be good to die

before comprehending this, because to know
life was like that—who could live with it,
even for a moment, knowing?

## Artisanal

Bring your own bread,
your breath, your own
mouth, open

all night. What wouldn't
I give to fill it?
I can't see

my breath yet catch it
again and again
like a magic coin

I use to buy myself
back from the self-
chamberbox,

that dank fromagerie,
again and again.
In its dark robe

worn open, the night—
blind prince
of the black cat—

has a page for us all.
What wouldn't I give
to fill it?

Such is the dreary
unwritten history
of hunger,

of what to say to stay
alive. We don't
write it down.

We can't keep it down.
Why bring it up?
Burn it all down.

Make it new. A real
writer makes do.
Famous last words.

Not even ink makes
the best ink; wine
better spreads a stain

and the mouth is
already wet—the better
to contain a fire

or catch a fish
or tell a story sharpening
the point of the last

meal—that incredible
question, star of dread.
My own words,

eaten like a cheese
requested for the death
of it, ending my sentence,

and the one after it.
There's always one after it.

**Wound**

As if to woo
not to wow.

I didn't dazzle like I expected
to. My body,

interracial & grumous,
either overly looked at

or totally overlooked.
My whole body isn't anything,

just a collection. What is
truly midmost me

is injury, an old one,
decrepit unreal thread opening

new self-holes, new tears
pronounced like *air*

not *fear.* The tear knits
back together,

stitches melt to keep
the wound soft, keep

a space which fills and fills
but never fills.

Disappointment's all right
& emptiness

can pulse weird useful energy.
But I'm most afraid

of panicked mind alone,
silent, in the end.

When fear becomes
an ability to split myself off

and my body is just another
kind of sourdough

hardening in the window
of the failing bakery.

Not even children stop
to look. They don't

want anything anymore,
hungry or not.

They too have had enough
of taking to fear

what gives of itself
without and to no end.

## Dress Form

Myself I'm like a dress my mother made
me, a fabric self split open with a sigh
as I grew and—bewildered or proud

or full of rage—patched with nicer
material than we'd had before. I got
the sense it was all wasted on me.

But a needle's sharp to pierce, is itself
pierced—so as to sew like I was taught.
Like I learned: no dress could ever be

beautiful or best if it had me in it.
I was the stain in a place we couldn't fix.
Having fallen on a slicer of some kind.

Double-seamed, scabbed over, a new body
pocket in the pattern. How to stitch up
that wound right into the clean vertical rip

in some on-sale flannelette?
I'd never again be cold. Skin's holey not holy.
In mad winter alone with drink, I think:

tattoo needles don't use thread but ink
to mark a place in this ever-moving skin
and that wound is ornament. But who

needs a mark to know what's marked?
I would pray to the dark in the dark.
But what did I ask for, what did I know

to ask for? Nonfatal wounds: they're there
when we die, deliquescent, vibrating like a drum
skin just after each beat moves off.

A part of music. A way a body keeps time,
is time's keeper, vigilant till time up and goes
to find another body. Another's warmth

and shelter. Or related injuries. Anyone
who hurts another was hurt that same way,
so how far back behind our backs do we go

to finally find the first hurt; whose finger
points to say, "You! You're the one who god
knows why started a cycle of unending pain,"

to someone's child in short pants?
A baby just torn a hole in her amnion swirl?
And what of me? I can't tell where my flesh

meets the rest of me, ragbag full of rags,
shot full of holes but that's just the way cotton
and silk and everything I said up till now looks

when it hits the air and is cried on. I'm so inside
out I evaporated entirely already as August does,
my actual dress shredded at the seams—

unsalvageable. Who would ever love me like this?
And just like that, I stopped thinking about it.
I agree to meet you at the ferry heading to a place

neither of us wants to go but both just said
*sure, I'll go… if you want!* We should turn back,
nobody said. Oh we should before it's too late,

nobody said again, insistent this time.

## How It Is

It isn't every day I can wrap my mind around it.
It being just what you'd think it is.

Not a thing or a condition of being but an extended
body holiday,

its movements are like dance but really more like fire

or cross-signals cut before anyone got there.
A flow-through mind,

a frank season so in love with some poor sister,

the long star rattling its universe like a snake.

If only I could gather eyefuls and throw them
curvingly with some accuracy at what I couldn't bear

to see before. Not just inside the body but inside
the insides, all the way in

till loved precious cells are cold neutral space again.

Can I get a witness? Can I get a witness
that way, if it were not so unreliable?

It again. It is always so unreliable.

It doesn't know what it is and is all right with that.

Isn't that strange?

It surely isn't me. I wouldn't be all right with not knowing.

Not it. That narrows it down I suppose. Not it.

Just keep saying that, eliminating. What's left

will will its way into it. Will scare me to pieces
which it will then not pick up

but leave for someone else to deal with. As I am
doing now with this mess here.

# II. CRUSHING LIKENESS

## Gay Pride Weekend, S.F., 1992

I forgot how lush and electrified
it was with you. The shaggy
fragrant zaps continually passing
back and forth, my fingertip
to your clavicle, or your wrist
rubbing mine to share gardenia
oil. We so purred like dragonflies
we kept the mosquitoes away
and the conversation was heavy,
mother-lacerated childhoods
and the sad way we'd both
been both ignored and touched
badly. Knowing that being
fierce and proud and out and
loud was just a bright new way
to be needy. *Please listen to me*, oh
what a buzz! *you're the only one
I can tell.* Even with no secret,
I could come close to your ear
with my mouth and that was
ecstasy, too. We barely touched
each other, we didn't have to
speak. The love we made leapt
to life like a cat in the space
between us (if there ever *was*
space between us), and looked
back at us through fog. Sure,
this was San Francisco, it was
often hard to see. But fog always
burned off, too, so we watched
this creature to see if it knew
what it was doing. It didn't.

## But I'm the Only One

*who'll walk across a fire for you,*
growled Melissa. That song
blared out from all four of
our bedrooms' tape decks,
often simultaneously, as if
that song were the only one
we all loved, the only one we
could agree on that summer
in the dyke loft, just when it
all started to change. Catherine
was moving out, to SoHo to
live with Melanie. So Shigi's
girlfriend DM took her room.
But not for long; they broke up
and Michelle moved in, shortly
after Cynthia came. *Tonight you
told me that you ache for something
new.* This was way before we'd
even dreamed we'd have to rent
out Shigi's office to Erin as a fifth
bedroom. Without Catherine we
couldn't afford the loft, but we
didn't know that yet. At the time
we thought everyone was poor
like us—we weren't the only ones.
We all smoked constantly, anyone
could afford to smoke back then.
Catherine bummed my last butt
but I know I saw her new carton
in the freezer. She didn't want
to open it yet, was trying to
cut back. This was before we
almost got the gas cut off, before

we lost electricity the first of
many times. After Justine had
been bullied out with her three
cats but Kristen—whom we
suspected was asexual and not
really lesbian—was still hanging
on even though she adopted yet
another cat into the loft without
asking. It was only one more,
she reasoned, but we already
had Seether, Amber, Balzac,
Gigli, and now Eva Luna.
Anna and Jackie came by,
they were friendly to me, but
Tjet and Julie weren't. T and J
were Clit Club. A and J were
literary. Then Michelle and
Shigi secretly slept together,
a disaster, and Cynthia got
kicked out for being bi and
then bringing a guy to the loft,
but that summer, before all that,
just after I'd been dumped by
the girl I'd moved to NYC
to be with, and just after I'd
invited my first college girl-
friend to come visit me
(not sure what I expected,
but she was the only one
who was willing to fly out)
but before I met Natira.
Our month-long affair
wasn't great but still pretty
damn good, she was the only
one I'd liked in a long time. I

hadn't met Sayeeda yet, at
Jackie's book party—Jackie
and Anna I think were broken
up by then. After Stefanie
but long before Tina, before
Jamie had even met Tina,
this song played everywhere,
every day, ceaselessly, so it
started to seem that *we* were
Melissa—that Cassandra—
foretelling in a ragged voice:
"*And I'm the only one who'll
drown in my desire for you.*"
We meant that we too were
willing to do anything to
prove we were the only one
for someone that one summer.

## To My Twenty-Six-Year-Old Self

You really are being such a poet,
aren't you? Ten dollars a week
is the food budget, and that's day-old

rolls for the freezer and looking for butts
and considering the offer from friends
who can get you a job at their strip club.

But you're too fat to be a stripper,
you say, starving down to nothing.
But this is the life of an artist, you say,

even when the electricity shuts down
and the cop on the corner offers you
cocaine if you'll fuck him,

but you need money, not drugs.
You write poems in the dark and tell
your friend you're dieting,

but later at the posh lesbian bar,
when she leaves her ten-dollar lychee
martini to go to the bathroom,

you steal it, and promise in your head
to write some lousy poem
for her later to pay her back.

## In This Economy

The economical ikebana
of the lesser octopus
is disarming,

a sextopus, holding
its intelligence
& ink

in a concentrate.
Not some sloppy octopus
who suddenly

freaks, so princessy, rich.
Driven to abstraction
not unlike flowers

dropping their petals
because petals are garbage
off the bloom,

not expensive anymore
thus going inside
to find meaning.

Cut the eyes, then, from
the cruel ikebana
of the racehorse—

if a leg breaks she can't
bear her own
weight,

long-blossomed head
turns to glue
and the fortune

zooms off like flies
from a carcass
when shooed.

The tripod fell
so I had to cast about
for my crutch

to walk over—my bad
left knee buckling—
to right it.

I want to take a picture
of the flowers
I arranged

after an ikebana class,
just one. I quit
quickly

but still hope to learn
to arrange beauty
classically.

Maybe I'm lazy, or
don't apply the rules
to myself,

or maybe "laze" is just
"zeal" rearranged,
as in my case.

Even now, the clock
we need to punch
out on is too far

away to plug in,
so power collects
in its hands.

## Why I Stayed, 1997–2001

Each time we moved to a new apartment,
and we did three times, I knew
I shouldn't, that I should

leave while I had the chance, but each
time we moved to a new apartment
we were desperate,

had been kicked out or priced out
and we only had one bed,
no savings, just friends

some of whom knew that you fractured
your hand punching through a wall,
inches from my head,

and some of whom were aware
that you threw things at me
when I said things

you didn't like, as if my words *were*
things I threw at you first.
It made sense to you.

I can't remember the bad things
I said—my self-serving
memory enraged

you, and why not: I always
remembered the bad
things you *did.*

And, yes, I do remember
everything you threw:
a chair

over our heads at a bar (Liz was
there), a mirror like a frisbee
aimed at my knees,

a carton of fried rice that splat
on the shade of our only
nice lamp, oil stains

patterned it with tiny bugs.
Also, you threw
me against a

wall, but you always said it was because
I made you so mad because
you loved me so much

and didn't want to lose me
that you'd lose control
instead and later

beg me to stay, that if I left you
it meant you would never
be loved and I couldn't

bear to have you think that
about either one of us.
I wasn't someone

who'd let herself be hit; I'd never
take that from a man. A man
would be a criminal

if he did what you did.
But you had been
hurt and all that

pain and anger needed more
time, and I made you so
crazy, I was so

stubborn and good at mean
words, what else were you
supposed to do?

You liked to raise your fist pretending
to hit me and then
half-smile when

I winced or cringed. It was important
that you had never *actually* hit me,
never punched me

with a closed fist: you'd only grabbed me
and choked me and flung me and made
dents in the wall next to me,

and narrowly missed me, but we knew you
meant to miss, never truly
meant to clobber me

on the head with something heavy,
something light, maybe,
like a book I loved.

When a woman you love hits you
on the head with a book
you love, is that love?

I was so ashamed and afraid someone
would find out about us, then I was
afraid and ashamed

people already knew but didn't know
what to do. Did I really think
this was a secret?

Not from the cops we called during two bad
fights or from Peggy who let you stay
with her rent-free that month

I kicked you out. You two had a blast.
But I couldn't pay the rent
on my own,

so you moved back in, triumphant,
Peggy still in love with you,
and you gloated about

how much money you'd saved.
Surrounded by friends,
whom could I tell?

Why would I tell anyone who didn't
already know us well enough
to already know?

If everyone knew, none of us said so.
We talked, all of us, almost
constantly, intimately,

so how did we keep ourselves so quiet?
You and I, together in this,
were alone with this,

alone among women who loved us.
The two of us never more alone
than when together.

# III. SO MUCH SYNTH

*Love is a stranger in an open car, to tempt you in and drive you far away.*

EURYTHMICS

## A Mix Tape: "Don't You (Forget About Me)"

> *Think of the tender things that we were working on.*
> SIMPLE MINDS

Such a delicious pain in the ass to make,
on a double deck if you were lucky,

otherwise you had to drop the needle
onto the precise groove as your left

index hit PLAY/RECORD, taking all
afternoon or many. Mistakes, thinking

too hard about what you wanted
to tell the person but couldn't say

any other way. It was always
"I love you," didn't you know?

Mix tape: private language, lost art,
first book, cri de coeur, X-ray, diary.

An exquisitely direct and sweet
misunderstanding. We weren't

fluent yet but we lived in its nation,
tense and sweaty for an anthem.

Receiving a mix tape could be major,
depending on from whom; giving one

to someone in public was a dilemma.
You had to practice. Would you say,

nonchalantly, "Oh, here, I made you
a mix tape?" By the lockers? In class?

Ugh! But giving it over in private
could be worse, especially arranging it.

You never picked the best song off
the album, definitely not the hit single.

The deeper the cut the deeper buried
your feelings for that person. You didn't

know? Not all lovesongs, though—
that would make you seem obsessed,

boring. They should know you're fun
and also funny and dark-hearted

and, importantly, unpredictable.
A "Blasphemous Rumours" for every

"Only You." And sexy! Though not
Prince's moaners—not "Erotic City,"

not "Darling Nikki"! But what?
Not Top 40, stylish, with a sly angle,

'70s funk, some Stevie Wonder, like you've
got background you don't really have.

As it records, you have to listen to each
song in its entirety, and in this way

you hear your favorite song with the ears
of your intended, as they hear it, new.

This was the best feeling of your young
life. Then the cold chill of suddenly hearing

in your third-favorite INXS song a lyric
you'd break out in hives over if you thought

they thought you thought that about them
when they heard it (*there's something*

*about you, girl, that makes me sweat*).
The only thing worse was the tape

running out a full minute before the end
of "There Is a Light That Never Goes Out."

You never got it right, not even once.
That was part of the mix tape's charm,

to your dismay. Did it ever win you
love? You never fell for anyone

else's mix either. Sometimes cool,
mostly was just someone else's

music in a case dense with tiny
handwriting to get all those titles in.

So much desire in those squeezed-in
letters. Not "Love me!" so much as

"Listen to me! Listen to me always!"
So that's really it, right? Maybe

you thought someday you'd make
a mix tape that your splendid friend,

your lucky star, your seventh stranger,
would take a pen to, punching in

the little plastic tabs which meant,
as you well know, it could never be

taped over again. They'd never use
your mix tape to make another mix tape

to give away, or to copy a friend's album
they didn't like enough to buy, joining all

the okay tapes in caddies stacked up a wall
or thrown in the backseat of the Datsun,

then in moving boxes, stored in parents'
garages, five for a buck at a yard sale,

buried in landfill, or, saddest of all,
discarded on the street, purple script

still aswirl on the white label FOR YOU—
JUST BECUZ. Shiny brown ribbon

tangled, strangled, never again to play
out what had to be said just that way.

# A Mix Tape: The Hit Singularities

## (Side A)

### 1. "LIKE A VIRGIN"—MADONNA

How to look out the window
and see something other

than the smear of purple apricot
that velvet sunset left

on my terrifying private sky,
in 1983?

### 2. "CRUEL SUMMER"—BANANARAMA

They didn't last the afternoon,
any of those three dates in a week,
three new guys I'd met.

I said yes to a drive to the beach,
to lunch at Sizzler and lunch
at a salad place.

I thought I was getting ready,
Sun In in my perm, but we could tell
by the silence.

It wasn't hungry or angry. Didn't
want a stronger stranger,
or even dessert.

Just caressed everything hopeless
with no muscles at all. Thanks!
See you in school.

### 3. "LET'S GO CRAZY"—PRINCE

Tonight's hemophiliac moon
(talented cheat) is brilliant

in the role of understudy
to the sometimes mad eye of Venus.

Or:

Being a smart girl who wants
to be in love is like breaking a leg

in a boring accident (sidewalk trip)
but the wound gets a disease (gangrene)

so everyone looks at you funny
but they don't really notice you.

### 4. "NOBODY'S DIARY"—YAZ

How do I deceive myself?
Do I act my happiness?

Am I good at acting it?
I live in a large box of air

playing records so unhappily.
I can't forget how you looked

at me, like I wasn't me and you
weren't you. How to change?

How to change everything
into everything you like?

## 5. "HOW SOON IS NOW"—THE SMITHS

Blood in the mouth
is so familiar, metal

in liquid form come
up to nourish source.

So we put to lips what
cuts us: paper, wood,

wire, knife, teeth.
I bite my tongue in two

when I smell your hair,
that Aqua Net.  When

will I know the smallest
hair? The softer things?

## 6. "YOU SPIN ME ROUND (LIKE A RECORD)"—DEAD OR ALIVE

Words: the berries of the cosmos,
plucked from their system

then changed beyond belief
because you don't believe me.

**(Side B)**

1. "DO YOU REALLY WANT TO HURT ME"—CULTURE CLUB

Against ourselves
we stand no chance—
we chop our wood,
jack our trades, gas
our cars, shave our heads
bare in solidarity with
not dying. We are
the miracle meat.
Sandwiches nobody
buys, wrapped in plastic
on display against
our wishes against
ourselves again.

2. "I RAN (SO FAR AWAY)"—A FLOCK OF SEAGULLS

I ran away only to prove
I chose my next move somehow.

Really you did not lose me:
you walked away. I sat there waiting

but you were gone. Only then did I run,
to salvage a mile or two of my own.

I don't know how much of my own story
is true and what I've had to believe.

Really I think I just sat there self-thinking
the same cruel sentences:

*You fool yourself, you do. And you know it, liar.*
I couldn't get away.

3. "HERE COMES THE RAIN AGAIN"—EURYTHMICS

No kind Nana
with papery hands to click
her knitting needles

and tell you that memory
itself used to have memory.
This wet dump doesn't

remember falling year
after year, but it did, does,
the very same stuff.

Water is One, to Old Earth-
Sky, even if we divide it
by tasks, titles, time.

4. "WORDS"—MISSING PERSONS

*Do you hear me? Do you care?*


If words were material
and not ether, ink, rivulet
of breath in space,

they'd have a hand-stitched
quality, each a starsplat
of sleep on a plain white

tight cotton sheet that robots
wove on their industrial looms.
They want us comfortable.

## 5. "NEW MOON ON MONDAY"—DURAN DURAN

Changeling starlings landing
on a line of verse or vine of voice

so singular

it's not inhuman but unihuman.
Simon says he's synced

to a perfect keyboard,
there's truth in synth.

That's what synth means:
to make true. An everglow

lost among the speechless.
Le bon mot swallows the night.

## 6. "(KEEP FEELING) FASCINATION"—THE HUMAN LEAGUE

I'm blinded by vision, like an artist
who paints miniature landscapes
and portraits on a grain of sand
using a microscope and tweezers,

who yells "Fuck!" when the tiny
brush with its single mousehair slips
and ruins the mountaintop the artist
has been scaling all morning, hoping

to peak by lunch. It was never going
to be a masterpiece, we know that,
but it does hold fast whatever art is in us,
that thing that blooms like failure and is.

## Is There Something I Should Know?

> *I know you're watching me every minute of the day yeah.*
> *I've seen the signs and the looks and the pictures.*
> *They give your game away yeah.*
>
> *There's a dream that strings the road*
> *With broken glass for us to hold,*
> *And I cut so far before I had to say:*
> *Please please tell me now!*
>
> DURAN DURAN

If I were fourteen again, I wouldn't be in this situation now,
trying to write without a pen. Isn't blood a woman's ink?

Back then, whatever I scratched into my well-filled,
ill-hid diary was my existence, and those scribblings—

fast as I could think, or slow as if carving a spell—
formed the outer periphery of me, the inner lining.

The rest of me: juice, some sponge,
electricity like synth riffs not interested in bringing light.

Sometimes I just dumped rage and hurt, yearning
for finer feelings, not the indignities I suffered.

But if I suffered sharply, I could scarcely trace it soft:
"You think you're pretty, dork?" spat at me at school

transcribed as: "Swirling Ugly Vortex. Stupid Me!"
alone in my room later. I scrounged for the words,

keeping the scope of it all very open, universal,
somehow dramatizing *and* minimizing.

"The worst thing in the whole world
is that nobody cares, not even me!!!"

Who was I kidding? Even in my private diary
I performed myself to an audience of one, no one.

A stock character playing to an empty house,
though I'd no theater experience at all.

I lied outright, wrote daydreams as if true,
was all-knowing and exquisite, simultaneously

the worst person ever to have lived. Adolescence
is all absolutes: if bad, one must be the very worst

to avoid being mistaken for average.
To be ordinary was just being invisible,

and surely slow naked death by ants hurts less than that.
The middle was always for losers. The middle seat,

the middle-aged, the middle child, the middle finger,
middle school, middling.

I remember writing: "One thing I know
I definitely am not is: a totally bizarre person."

Only a few years later my entire persona
so craved a real and lasting bizarreness, I fashioned

it out of my relentless wholesomeness,
easily, actually, because hallucinogens are great

for making you think you actually are weird.
But that came later. In junior high I was a kid

under the impression I was supposed to act
grown up, and that meant knowing who I was

and how groups started or shaped, like on the bus
or at lockers if you didn't go to the same grade school

as a lot of people who all knew each other, and what
to wear and how my own body worked at least.

At least how to become friends with people
I liked without just mimicking them and trying

to figure out how to join their group? But how?
And boys could tease you or yell anything, do

anything. How'd you know where you stood?
Every scene—lunch, P.E., English—had different rules,

invisible: they changed depending on who had power.
That was never you. You couldn't just be yourself anywhere.

There was an amazing story in me, one that I would live
powerfully, in wet velvet poetry: *And you wanted*

*to dance so I asked you to dance, but fear is in your soul…*
the voice of Simon Le Bon permeated all those

new cells, the bloody ones, the ripenings, and I knew
his love was deep. Too deep, maybe, hard to know what

anything he sang meant. He was also a little whiny.
The perfect pretty pout of John Taylor, however,

with that sunken chest—fetishized forever after that—
was New Romantic, graceful, not quite as lurid

with makeup as Nick Rhodes but still breathtaking
in girlish man-ness. Perfect perfect,

all absorbed in brooding sounds and slow,
distant love that maybe insinuated sex

but was more like helpless desire, a beautiful
man mooning over… me? Much emotional

clutching of said sunken treasure before
glamorously running down the wet

tarmac in a flapping linen suit to catch a plane
to the next *some people call it a one-night stand*

*but we can call it paradise.* Yes, I'd be left, newly
a woman, languid and a little tearful thinking

about my erotic awakening in the bungalow
by really any of Duran Duran except Andy.

※ ※

Before pubescence's acrid synthesis—those 700 days—
I was a kid: all glossy grubby greatness, jumping through

sprinklers, full-tilt rollerskating, running down
the street while running my mouth, just as often

riveted to the silent endlessness
demanded by a beautiful or terrifying story: I'd hide

and lose and seek and find myself in every page:
laughing, rereading and then re-rereading

out loud, disbelieving the details till my system
could absorb them like the nutrients they were.

Sara Crewe was so kind I'd disappear into her
and only a perfect girl remained.

Surely I'd have adored her in silks or in rags.
How I yearned to show her that I, too, knew

that being good meant to *love goodness* and
not just act nice to get what I wanted.

In *Maggie Adams, Dancer,* I'd be Joyce—sure, okay.
I didn't mind! The slightly chunky ballerina

ever-cast as the gingerbread lady or Rat King,
never Sugar Plum. I would tend the sad traumas

of Maggie, slender and spotless, just trying her best
against that evil wall of perfection

she kept slamming her lithe body against.
Maggie's problems didn't make you pity her,

unlike Lupe, the religious Latina who was anorexic
and died! Or Joyce, who predictably tanked because

of her wrong body type. She was only fooling
herself. Maggie had snags that made you admire her.

The kind of protagonist whose beauty and high-spirited
intelligence are cast as flaws: she hates her gorgeous,

"unruly" red corkscrew curls and her "too long" legs,
her mortifying but adorable blushing, a temper

that flares at unfairness, her embarrassing way
of always blurting out helpful truths that move

the plot along, deepening and developing
all the supporting characters.

By the end of *Maggie Adams,* my 700 days were well
underway. My love for Maggie changed

and was now, I suspected, unwholesome. God would
have frowned, or so the dogma went then.

Sure it seemed okay to *think* any old thoughts,
especially if you didn't *say* anything, but the problem

with God is that he was supposedly there in your
thoughts already, could hear them. So why pray?

I wondered. If he can already hear me, aren't all
my thoughts, then, even the sexy ones, prayer?

And how could he understand what I was thinking
about Maggie if he hadn't read the book?

Whoever heard of God reading? Like curled
up on the sectional reading about teen ballerinas

or snooping in a twelve-year-old's diary?
Anything that happened between those covers,

on those sheets of paper, was safe, and my thoughts
were protected from God's snooping.

It wasn't just Maggie, not only kind and beautiful
white girls—though that's who I usually fell for,

and underdogs, too. I could love so variously
so many kinds of people in books,

not just the victim in *Blubber* but her tormentors,
the ignored twin Wheeze, the boy in the peach,

the boy who masturbated, strong weird Anastasia,
Casey Child of the Owl, Deenie with scoliosis,

the girl with anorexia, the girl who was raped,
the girl who didn't speak, the girls who died.

Heathcliff and Cathy, both, of course, though
Cathy less. She didn't deserve Original Goth Guy

and was a goody-goody. I hoped one day I'd see
someone in real life and have that "love"-like feeling

(*I try to discover a little something to make me sweeter*),
whisper, "It's happened!" and touch myself in awe:

"This is the me it happened to!"
(*Oh baby refrain from breaking my heart!*)

Me, once sick or strange or poor or unlucky,
somehow now utterly loved, absolutely chosen,

lifted out of dreary life in our subdivision,
sleeping well through the occasional engine

revving out of control down our through-road.
During the 700 days I began to understand

that when love happened, I'd become real.
(*I'm so in love with you, I'll be forever blue.*)

I wouldn't be living as one of "us." Part of an old family.
This sad unit started by them, my parents,

which had zero logic and seemed to have nothing
to do with me. (*That you give me no reason*

*why you're making me work so hard!*) Sometimes what's good
for everyone forced each individual to act

compensatorily (*that you give me no*),
nobody getting what they wanted (*that you give me no*).

I wanted to yell, jump, skate, sing, write, rant!
I wanted to be loved, to love, to find gentleness

and sexy strength and not be stuck being me
(*Soul, I hear you calling*),

to somehow lift the ME up into some other world
where someone (who? this was the great mystery)

might lose himself (herself?) in me (*Oh baby please!*),
the heroine of this most wonderful story.

Such a satisfying story that I wouldn't have to diet
or worry about my clothes or how awkward my jokes were

(*that you give me no*). My quotations were always in character,
endearing, and if I was weird, that was part

of what made me so much fun to read, "quirky" (*that you
give me no*), my unpredictability and sweetness and nuzzly,

irrepressible oddness and charisma. My inelegance
transformed into a set of classic and eternal qualities

propelling the story to greatness. (*Give a little respect. To. Me!*)
Without that story, I just said stupid things

that killed me late at night, squirming at the memory
of my idiocy. I told Jenny her hair was like *straw?*

I knew she was mean but I thought she was stupid
enough to take it as a compliment. But she detected

the intended insult and hissed at me.
Now she knows how I really feel about her,

and I'm just as mean as her, but obviously dumber.
(*Give a little respect! To! ME!*)

This feeling of being out of control of what I said
was happening more frequently.

I used to be able to say exactly what I wanted,
often disastrously ("I don't want to leave the mall,"

for example, I said once when I was seven-ish.
I must have been really bad, impossible,

because my mom drove away and left me there
outside wandering the concrete planters.

I was scared. She didn't come back for a long time.
I pretended to be interested in the shrubbery,

acting like I didn't care, especially when I saw her
car pull up. I got in, hoping I seemed indifferent.

I didn't want her to know I was scared. Was I?
Why did I want to stay at the mall anyway?)

"I want to see a movie with Lisa H.! Her mom's driving!"
"I don't want to go to Japanese school!"

"I hate piano lessons!" and overruled again
and again until finally I wasn't. And decades later

I mourn the unlearned Japanese language and the piano.
What did I know about what I wanted?

What I said I wanted was ignored, until finally
a parent got fed up with hearing me whine

and then it was, "Fine! You don't want to go,
you don't have to go. Your grandmother wanted

you to learn piano, but fine! You win."
That it was Nana who wanted us to learn piano

seemed to confirm how pointless that would be.
When we saw her once or twice a year, she'd

again say that once we learned to play the piano,
we'd be the "belles of the ball!"

But I was into Duran Duran and Madonna and Prince.
Not to mention Dead or Alive and Yaz and Erasure.

I was into the future. So much synth. So much
silvery, zingy computer music: *I wouldn't say that*

*you were ruthless or right. I couldn't see from so far.*
Oh god, is there any music as good as what you heard

at fourteen? It never occurred to me that the music
forever imprinted on Nana's young psyche

was the piano, played by a girl luckier and richer than she.
The one girl loved enough to be given lessons

was the source of teen joy and envy in her group,
and she wished this glory for us. Of course it didn't occur

to me. (How could Nana have been a teenager?)
I was accustomed to being ignored (unfairly, I thought)

and then listened to (but what did I know?)
at the wrong times, almost, it seemed, at precisely

the wrong times, like how I always choose the polar
opposite direction of where I am supposed to go,

if I am going by instinct. (*Was I chasing after rainbows?*
*One thing for sure you never answered when I ca-a-alled.*)

Or how it feels when forced to call a side of a coin:
heads is the winner's call but it loses as often as tails,

while tails is the countermove which should have
some advantage but doesn't. When you get your call

it feels like just luck, but when you don't it's failure.
This is the feeling of having duped yourself into thinking

you had some control over that awful double-edged
mystery we call "chance." Randomness or opportunity.

Both were terrifying. *But I still can feel those splinters of ice.*
*I look through the eyes of a stranger.*

I remember convincing myself, when I was thirteen,
that I hadn't "really" gotten my period. This was because

I'd only gotten it once, then twice, then three times,
and it seemed unreal it'd be here to stay.

My first menstruation (which was never what we called it
even once) came a month before I turned thirteen, and it felt

too fast to be twelve with it. I knew I wasn't "a woman"
but a big kid still not allowed to say bad words,

yet was suddenly supposed to be fluent in a rough
and dirty language now that I had "the curse"

and was "on the rag." Even if we said it cute ("riding
the little white surfboard"), I thought it was gross

to get it at twelve. Where did I get that idea?
I knew from *Are You There God? It's Me, Margaret*

that you were supposed to pray, hope, and wait for it,
celebrate it, tell everyone in your family.

I thought mine was too brown, poop-like, hardly a
glamorous womanly thing I'd read about in a great book!

It didn't seem ladylike or sexy at all. It was just scary
and messy and had to be hidden from everyone

because everyone knew it was totally disgusting.
If you ever got your period at school in such a way

that anyone knew, you'd never get over the humiliation.
You'd have to convince your parents to move.

This scenario terrorized us. No way was I ready
to handle such a delicate social secret.

Whether anyone else was, who knew?
We couldn't talk about it because some people

hadn't gotten it yet and were shy about that, others shy
because they did and didn't want anyone to know.

You weren't supposed to ask. *For rumors in the wake*
*of such a lonely crowd, trading in my shelter for danger.*

Every month it felt like some sordid and revolting thing
was happening to me, and it was.

No one discussed it or acknowledged it
even though we ALL READ THE JUDY BLUME.

Basically, all the stories I'd read or heard about
what it was really like to become a woman

made me rather expect a kind of slow, gorgeous
liquefaction after which I'd emerge a cross

between Jessica Rabbit and Denise Huxtable
except that I was half-Japanese, and so neither fit,

but nothing fit anyway. Not Dorothy Gale or Coco
from *Fame* or Strawberry Shortcake

(*I'm changing my name just as the sun goes down,*
*walking away like a stranger*) or Cyndi Lauper

or Punky Brewster or Smurfette or Madonna
or, well that's it. Who else was there to shadow?

(...*such a lonely crowd*) Cartoon, fashion plate,
tragedy, infantile aesthete, video clown, sex paradox.

Dimensions of two, not three.
Never four. Oh how time traveled through a mind

and body shifting from Anne of Green Gables
to Samantha Fox in 700 days.

For the better part of a year, I kept my arms crossed
in front of my chest as if in a bad mood,

hoping no one would see how my swollen mushroom
nipples poked out my shirt. I was afraid

of a bra, convinced that everyone would see
my straps and know that I was aware I had breasts

and that I knew what it was like to have them,
to "shoulder" that responsibility, understand all

the jokes that went along with them. Imperative to hide
your period; impossible to hide your breasts.

My mom begged me to wear my 32AA to school,
but I wore three shirts instead. It was like falling off a cliff

in the dark. I hit the ground in seventh grade,
at a new school where all the eighth graders wore bras,

where suddenly lack of bra straps would be
the source of embarrassment. Poor Shannon,

my best friend who was still flat: six months ago
I'd prayed to be like her, and now I felt sorry for her.

She looked so short and skinny and small,
like a fourth grader!  But I had other worries:

the dark hair on my lower legs nobody else
seemed to have, and which my short sweatsocks

didn't cover during drill team/gym,
though I pulled them up as high as I could.

Pure misery, those tiny blue shorts—
but not that tiny, I had to get the Mediums,

which made me feel fat when another Shannon
and a Lori got Extra Extra-Small, but okay when

a Tahnya and a Kathleen got Extra Extra-Large.
How could my size, exactly in the middle,

make it seem I was both extremes?
In middle school, running in the middle of the pack

in the middle of the road, now offered precious
invisibility that wasn't as safe as it seemed.

You could easily become nobody.
And why was there no such size as Extra Medium?

Nobody showered, because people would see you
naked. Some Ramona wasn't even wearing a bra

at *this* point, just a little girl's undershirt with a bow.
We weren't mean. We didn't have to be.

She curled over in self-loathing, yanking her sweater
on, her jeans, face a tomato hurled at herself.

Oh god seventh grade! Just staring at my pale leg
and my dark hairs. I knew my mom wouldn't let me shave,

just like she wouldn't let me use tampons, only pads.
Not that I asked. I was too embarrassed to ask:

she just bought pads for me, a new box in my underwear
drawer every month, while there was always a box of Playtex

plastic tampons on the toilet tank in her bathroom.
I tried one, stuck it up there and couldn't feel a thing.

Amazing! But I was confused to see blood running
down my leg. So I read the directions. Ohhhh!

You stick the tampon in, holding on to just one tube, push
the bottom tube into the first, and pull BOTH plastic parts out

and put them in the trash! You inject yourself with the tampon!
OHHH! You really did have to read the directions.

I was never going to figure that out myself.
Anyway, tampons were way better because you

couldn't see them and they didn't slip, but you also
didn't know whether they were full or not. So?????????????

Accidents no matter what. After stealing enough mom-pons,
my mom finally bought me my own Slender Regulars,

which I knew from magazines were for teens.
Those teens looked so glossy, their fluids regulated;

they rode on sparkling streams of lovely teenage cuteness.
Their periods undetectable, their gym shorts Extra Small,

their legs either hairless by nature
or by their mom's permission, their skin flawless

and their head-hair flowing. I stared at them in magazines;
the ones I got were *Young Miss* and *Seventeen.*

Their fluidity seemed to carry them straight to stardom,
adored by all. My chunky fluids got on my sheets.

My greasy bangs covering my eyes, I stared at myself
in the mirror: *What kind of butt is that? It doesn't seem… right.*

I don't know how I convinced my mom to let me
shave my legs. I only remember that the problem

disappeared, so she must have let me. At some point,
my younger sister stole a razor, my mom's or mine,

I'm not sure, and sliced up her shin in the bath.
Long strips of skin lay in the tub after

our parents took her to the hospital.
It looked worse than it was (the inverse of the usual),

and I recall them looking like beige carrot peels
turning brown. She'd felt the same desperation I did.

It hadn't occurred to me anyone but me could have it.
The thing is: no one looked us in the eye and told us

anything (*Please please tell me now!*), and maybe
we wouldn't have listened (*Is there something I should know?*)

and maybe reading about puberty in pamphlets
was somewhat effective since we were such good readers,

but pamphlets either gave numbered instructions:
    (1) Read instructions before use.

(2) Raise one foot up on the toilet as illustrated
or talked in euphemisms: "feeling like a lady

during your special time!" one said. Another: "Pretty is
as pretty does!" Pretty does what? I thought.

Pretty IS what? What could that possibly mean?
If even the grown-ups were too embarrassed to talk

to us about blood and mess and cramps and hormones,
it must be really bad. As bad as divorce or cancer—

that level of hush, with whispers around the people
involved. Our bodies' changes were kept secret

from us alone; everyone else could see. (*People stare and
cross the road from me.*) But I had my secrets, too.

Wanting to be wanted by someone I wanted.
(*Do you feel the same 'cuz you don't let it show*)

How complicated that desire turned out to be, now,
with this weird new thing: being wanted by those

I didn't want at all, or at least I didn't think so,
but how to know how to know who you want?

Aside from knowing for sure that if John Taylor
could carry you off with those skinny arms of his

you'd totally do it, who in real life was there to like?
You might get laughed at no matter who you picked,

unless he picked you. But that's not you wanting
who you want, right? And by "wanting" what

do you mean?  You're a good girl, you have to be nice—
if you're not, the consequences are not so nice:

you've seen a loudmouthed girl elbowed in the tits
by a boy in a laughing group. She got quieter, "nicer"—

so even when someone's totally off-the-charts rude,
lewd, or crude, the only known response is a polite one.

The rude ones count on this, of course.
Ancient ploy: convince young girls they lack

some undisclosed quality of such importance
it's the only thing men and boys will ever want

them for, to persuade them they're so defective
they're lucky he's a cool guy who accepts all

the flaws no one else would put up with, a nice
guy who wants to help them feel beautiful

by inserting his penis, often without warning,
into their precious young bodies and use them,

their whole dear romantic trusting selves,
to get his pleasure from their orifice, which

is what he spent all that energy trying to procure,
even though he claimed he had better

things to do. He thinks he's a cool customer
in an antiques store who sees a priceless treasure

and knows he can convince the seller it's a piece
of junk, dented and dirty, she's lucky to get five

bucks for it. He's the only one who understands
this to be a deal, a sale, a score.

A fourteen-year-old girl doesn't have any idea how rare
her own body is. She's only ever lingered over its flaws,

ever since childhood ended,
around 524 days ago, eternity in reverse.

She thinks it is worth nothing; she's not a place
where treasures can be bought cheap or stolen.

She thinks it's kind of sweet that someone noticed
her, that maybe it's a sign she's lovable after all.

Because he's convinced her that his desire is hers,
and that being "fuckable" is a compliment.

What I learned at fourteen was that there was never a short
supply of boys twelve years old, men of seventy,

every age in between, who were interested and willing
and didn't even need to be asked to give an opinion

on my fuckability. And no matter what I thought of *them*,
it was *their* opinion that would never be omitted

in the final tally of my total worth.
And that nowhere in the world would my opinion

of *their* fuckability (what a joke!) ever be considered
relevant in any circumstance or for any reason.

I knew that men could walk past me and call me "slut"
and "nice-tits" and "oriental pussy" and I couldn't even

complain about it because it was embarrassing,
and furthermore, bragging!

Yes! If you told anyone, that person gave you a weird,
pinched look as if you'd just given yourself

this lewd compliment and were fishing for more.
If you told anyone that some fifty-year-old man

waggled his tongue at you out his car window
then stuck his index finger though a hole he'd made

with his other hand ("Then how was he steering?"
someone was sure to ask with a doubting smirk),

driving slow past you as you walked on the highway
to the mall, you were surely making it up.

And it just made you look bad if you said it,
as if saying it was what made it really happen.

If you told anyone your own age that a big, tall guy
a little older than you whispered, "I bet you're slutty,"

your friends would ask how he knew you (ha ha!)
so well. (You're a virgin, haven't even kissed.)

Because the only person you could tell was another
girl like you, who was so confused about what it all meant

that we figured it must have meant nothing, since
nothing was done about it and nothing about it mattered.

If you told your mom, you wouldn't
be able to go anywhere or wear anything halfway cool.

No peach lipgloss. No two-inch Cherokee sandals, on which I
learned to balance the height of a heel and the price of the pair

with social correctness and mom's all-important okay.
Because she was buying. And she was short so she was okay

generally with a little heel height even if you were fourteen.
But if you told your mom, you'd be in Mary Janes

and so would your twelve-year-old sister. If you told your dad,
well, this was unthinkable. You could never tell your dad.

Telling your dad meant you were failing.
A baby bird crushed underfoot after that first

unsuccessful leap from the nest. Maybe it meant
something was wrong with the nest or the branch

was too high, but no one ever thought that.
You were just a loser.

It hurt when a man yelled out of a car but there was no
way to feel it. There was no synapse connecting

wound to brain, no way to know where it hurt or why.
It was inward, and if no one noticed, it just as well

didn't happen. The wound was never compared
to what might have blossomed there in a world where men

did not throw cruel, vicious "compliments" at young girls;
the wound was only ever compared to the worst-

case scenario: the car stopping, the duct tape and the trunk.
You didn't even have to say the word *rape*. It was

assumed that's what the crime would be. What other
imaginable thing could an unknown man in a car want with you?

Your money? Your extorted promise to renew
the municipal contract for the mob's energy company?

Revenge for turning down his nephew for prom date?
Just looking for someone to talk to?

There's nothing else a fourteen-year-old has that anyone would
want enough to commit a crime for. So you should be happy

you just got yelled at. You should feel relieved and lucky
and happy that the only thing that you are valued for

was not taken by force and was instead merely jeered at
and threatened. When you learn that you are supposed

to feel lucky and happy because you weren't raped and killed,
you are already, in this, being truly brutally hurt

in a central, deep, and formative place. This is never admitted.
This is never permitted acknowledgment.

If you say this, someone will refute it. So I will say it here.
We can't know the extent of the damage caused

by the constant threat of rape: the mutations, the atrophy,
emptiness, self-mutilation, isolation, fear, flying fucks,

can seem defensive, bitchy, *loca*, now you are too damaged
to have any say-so. So no wonder bad things happen.

Everything you say is crazy. Even if nothing bad ever happens
to you, whatever you could have been if not for this damage

isn't real or considered valuable, so losing it is not a loss.
You never matter. Not your safety today or your potential.

It never matters that every experience you'll ever have
will be curtailed, limited, cut, and that you will participate

in that with every sentence you speak ending in a question
so as not to anger anyone who needs to be right?

You know that being right isn't worth being assaulted and killed?
You learned it young? Maybe it kept you alive?

When you are fourteen and trying to become yourself
and you learn this self is quickly becoming a target

but you can't tell anyone, you dodge and go fast, get it over with,
you hurt yourself first so no one can do it to you; you choose

to give your virginity to the first person who seems to be
the kind of person who wouldn't take it

in a mean way. You don't know if you felt anything.
You don't know if you liked it, or him.

He's cute, maybe, but ugh. Not really. You don't even recognize
when you feel revulsion for him that this is not the same

feeling as your near-constant disgust of yourself. It feels the same:
something's wrong with you and the world is normal.

※      ※

Surely, though, once the 700 days are thousands of days
past, eventually, we'd be grown women, be in charge,

like in college! It would surely be better. Would turn
into the fun kind of love and romance and lust

that both the lovers liked! Leave way behind the New
Romantics, so embarrassing I even liked them,

and be cool enough to synthesize the harsher stuff,
the industrial clang of Ministry and New Order

with the warm/cold currents of R.E.M and Everything

But The Girl, and the poetry and politics of Public

Enemy, and the Beastie Boys' goofball misogyny rap
(being cool meant enduring those cruel lyrics if

you wanted to hang out) and Pixies obsession,
and pretending to like the Butthole Surfers,

swept away for real by L7 and K.D. and Ani
and Deee-Lite and the encroaching sponge of grunge.

So there were more options, plenty of ways
to get it right, right? Reggae, techno, rap, rock.

If a girl was good enough, and pretty enough, sexy
in the way that could earn the right kind of attention,

she might attract a guy who treated her special,
as a complicated and exciting human being who

just happened to be sexy in the way that could
earn this right kind of attention.

This was the goal of the game.
This game with the vibe of a Roman gladiator stadium.

It was real life, this game, but you still had to play it.
If you won, you got to keep your body.

If you lost, you lost everything: your confidence,
your easy laughter, your ability to look in the mirror

and feel beautiful, your secret language, your eros,
your sense of humor, your flamboyant clothing style,

your enthusiasm for side-projects or for developing
your weaker arts, your lust, your late nights

alone without fear, your trust, your tipsy nights
dancing with friends, your friendships, your grades,

your way of flirting, your strange ability to shoot milk
out of your nose if there is sufficient social pressure,

your scholarship, your self-respect, your kindness,
your nights without nightmares, your openness,

your sense that you could choose or do what you wanted
and loved to do, your all and your future all.

Your dreams of having desire, believing that could
be relevant, and of fooling around, getting excited,

maybe falling for someone and wanting them,
and being wanted without being used by someone

who knows exactly how to use you.
Your story. The book of your life,

just the way you wanted to tell it, in the full
range of your voice. Your jumping, your singing,

your skating, your ranting, your shout of joy
in the sprinklers. That growing voice,

finding new timbre and tendency and tone.
Not just strong and smart but the chance

to quaver, too. Not just power—finding softness
and ambivalence and vigor and questions.

That voice, now rare, now quiet, keeps it in.
When it comes out, it's all question, all mark.

Your hope of being the brave and fierce
and loving and authentic protagonist

of the kind of story you wanted to read,
the story you wanted to live—none of that happened.

Or if it did, no one listened anyway, so why
say anything? But yours is not a story like this.

This is not a book anyone wants to read;
that's not a likable character, nothing she does

is believable. She's passive, lets herself
be a victim, where's her fire, her fight?

Why isn't she like Katniss, Hermione, Jo March,
Laura Ingalls, Lyra, Cowslip, Ramona, Heidi, Scout?

Unlike them, credible and realistic heroines,
she's not convincing. She's nothing like me.

Hers is not a voice you want to hear, nothing
she says matters, she's not a person you want

to have to listen to, page after page after page,
she's not real. I can't relate. She's not me,

she could never be me. That girl's long gone.
That girl didn't make it. No way that girl's

gonna make it. This isn't even a story.
My story's not here. Not even mine anymore—

I'm not even sure anything happened to me.
Or to whom everything happened.

# IV. SECRETS SEE ME COMING

## Life's Work

The round, white knob
on the dresser drawer—
a pull, it can be called—
is loose, becoming unscrewed
from itself. To tighten it,
I must empty the drawer
of the clothes nobody's ever
worn and nobody will ever
like, find the screwdriver
I don't think I've ever used,
or even have anymore,
use it with both hands, one
outside the drawer to steady
the pull and one inside
to screw it. We used to say
that all the time to joke
we'd given up: "Screw it!"
But we hadn't. Given up,
that is. Now here I am,
still at it. I talk about poems
for a living, and I bake muffins,
bran with raisin puree instead
of sugar and I'm chapped
when no one eats them.
These details make it seem
like real life, this one spent
managing and wrangling
as much as mothering, writing
lists and e-mails instead of poems.
Home is where we stay safe
and warm, yet keep it hot
and ever wanting it
to be a beautiful story as well

as real and aware of pain,
a story where a little jumble's
okay but where things should
kind of cohere as best they can,
and with that modest goal
I try to attend to things
like drawer pulls. I don't
want it to fall off and get
lost forever. A couple of twists
of the screwdriver and I can
feel how the slightly spongy
wood gives, compresses,
and now the knob is tight.
The dresser, however,
is on a bit of a slant, so
that drawer tends to fall
open on its own anyway.
Whenever I walk past it
I'm always pushing it
closed with my knee.

**Family Visit Vouchers**

Everyone stopped eating so much
pasta, as if it all had always been one
long noodle that finally concluded.

That's no way to spend the holidays.
So we don't spend them, as a group, anymore.
We save them like expired coupons

in the junk drawer, pushed back
behind the twist ties and the off-brand
batteries. Come on! Coupons?

Yes, coupons. Why so surprising?
You are only aware that someone
(you've known your entire life) cut them out

(of the circular with the family scissors)
because here they are, forsaken,
intact, irredeemable at no cost to you.

## Red Tulips, Then Asphodel

Was I ever truly happy, like some girl in a red tank top
eating sunlight in spring?

Hard to say. If flowers are symbols of emotions,
it's still hard to say.

What belongs, what goes, and which way. Did I once
feel like a tulip

bending gracefully toward its own root, its own death,
the lower my head

the more beautiful? Or was I ever showy like a peony
for one wild week,

sexed fully pink without blushing? What are emotions
anyway? Flowers die

not knowing. And yet our feelings lead us down that one
path we only ever take,

deceptively edged with bloom after bloom after bloom.

## Please Be Okay till Morning

How dangerous air could be if it broke
its pact with your fine little lungs—
just forgot its path a couple of minutes,

or the tractor trailer swinging
its back end into our lane, the rickety
scaffolding we're scooting under;

you with your powerful baby girl legs,
rocketing ahead and then fixed, meticulous,
on the sidewalk's cracks and gum stains.

You won't move on till you've questioned
every tree and flower, mother, sweeper,
toddler, dog, rock, and jogger on the street.

I have questions, too, quiet begging: No
lightning, all right? Not poison? Don't bite
her, don't hurt her, watch where you're going.

All the doors you want to try, I see them
swing out with knobs just the right height to
knock out your eye. Cars swerving onto

the sidewalk, drivers texting or heart-failed.
The fall on the sidewalk that isn't skinned knee
and the ritual choosing of the band-aid

but concussed, sleepy, a strangely
early bedtime, unusually late to wake up—
then find you cold at morning.

I say this only because I can't bear to say it;
it runs my mind day and night and night
and day. I am so afraid, always so afraid—

and I don't know if I should try to outrun
this fear, get way ahead so it can never find
me, or stop and stare it down,

stare into its great crack and insist
it recognize me: "Hello! Hello it's a nice day
isn't it Mr. Tree Fear? Mr. Car Fear?"

Should I open its door, meet its eyes, fall on
my knees, beseeching, head to floor,
*Please let her be okay till morning.*

Or stand guard, certain of my powers,
until I nod off, midprayer, then wake up
shaking from the worst dream, my shouts

are how I know lungs kept their vigil tonight
—fear's rhythm—fear that nothing more
mysterious than breath brings you

back to me each day. Let each day be the day
the driver doesn't look down at the text—bad news—
while turning the corner, stunned,

where we cross the street, on our way home,
radiant with dreamy leaps, your vital, mighty self,
bright hair whirling in that dangerous air.

## Simone at Age Three, Late Summer

Total astonishment, "Mommy! Look!
It's the moon!" Pointing to the silver

teacup balancing in blue late morning.
Then sternly: "In the daytime."

Her fingers cup her chin—a thinking
pose—she shakes her head solemnly

as if in disbelief, "It's very, very strange."
Looks at me again to confirm. "Yes,

Simone, it's mysterious. Now come on,
let's move along. We gotta get to school."

But she's still examining the sky. "Look,"
I say, "the leaves are just beginning to turn

brown and fall on the ground, see? That
means summer's almost over."

"I like this breeze." she says. "I want
to stay here in the shade. You can have

the sun, Mommy. I know you like it."
Protesting—"I like both"— I say, "But let's

keep walking." She sighs. "This wind
is so nice"; she closes her eyes and follows

my voice, her big toes already reaching
the edges of her scuffed gold sandals.

They only lasted two months. Already she's
forgotten she'd meant to monitor the day

moon, and we might get to Court Street
on time, or nearly so. "Summer's over,

the leaves fall in fall. The moon is strange,
very strange, but what season is the wind?"

**Never Ever**

Alarmed, today is a new dawn,
and that affair recurs daily like clockwork,

undone at dusk, when a new restaurant
emerges in the malnourished night.

We said it would be this way, once this became
the way it was. So in a way we were

waiting for it. I still haven't eaten, says the cook
in the kitchen. A compliant complaint.

I never eat, says the slender diner. It's slander,
and she's scared, like a bully, pushing

lettuce around. The cook can't look, blind with hunger
and anger. I told a waiter to wait

for me and I haven't seen him since. O it has been forty
minutes it has been forty years.

*Late* is a synonym for *dead,* which is a euphemism
for *ever. Ever* is a double-edged word,

at once itself and its own opposite: always
and always some other time.

In the category of *cleave,* then. To cut and to cling to,
somewhat mournfully.

That *C* won't let *leave* alone. Even so, forever's
now's never, and *remember* is just

the future occluded or dreaming. The day has come:
a dusty gust of disgusting August,

functioning as a people-mover. Maybe we're going
nowhere, but wherever I go

I see us everywhere. On occasions of fanciness
or out to eat. As if people, stark, now-ish

people themselves were the forever of nothing,
the everything of nobody,

the very same self of us all, after all, at long
last the first.

Thank you to the editors of the magazines and journals in which the following poems appeared: "Never Ever" on Academy of American Poets, Poem-A-Day (www. poets.org), "Mix Tape: Don't You (Forget About Me)" in *TheAwl*, "But I'm the Only One" in *The Literary Review*, "Mix Tape: The Hit Singularities" in *New England Review*, "I Have a Time Machine" in *The New Yorker*, "Life's Work" and "In This Economy" in *The Paris Review*, "Red Tulips, Then Asphodel" in *T Magazine*.

I'm grateful for the generosity of the Guggenheim Foundation, of the Corporation of Yaddo, and of the Radcliffe Institute for time, space, and support. Thank you to L. Samantha Chang at the University of Iowa Writers' Workshop, for the chance to teach a semester, and to my colleagues and students there. Wickham School and University Preschool took loving care of my kids, as did Megan Brummel (née Escher), Kiley Beck, Nicole Pietrzak, Bex Kwan, and Dana Jaye Cadman. Eliza Factor and Extreme Kids & Crew inspired me, and created community and supportive space for our family. Rebecca Pronsky's kindhearted vocal instruction released much of my voice: I wrote a lot of this book because I was taking lessons with her!

I'm so fortunate to be part of the M.F.A. and English departments of Rutgers University–Newark, and I'm grateful for the guidance and friendship of Jayne Anne Phillips, Alice Elliott Dark, Fran Bartkowski, and Jan Lewis. My RU–N students are astonishing and brilliant, and I'm thankful to them for making me walk my talk as a teaching poet.

Thank you to Copper Canyon Press: Michael Wiegers, Joseph Bednarik, Tonaya Craft, and dazzling Kelly Forsythe. Extraordinary readers/friends who helped this manuscript come together, your insights, precision, and generosity mean the world to me: Robyn Schiff, Nick Twemlow, Rigoberto González, and Merrill Feitell. As always, Craig Teicher, my love and long-suffering reader of works-in-progress: I'm so lucky we're in this together.

Cal, you're not in this book much (though you were the star of the last one), but you are an integral part of everything I do, so you are here in it anyway, a force of love and sweetness. Simone, you are the inspiration for so many of these poems. I want the world to be safer for you. Your 700 days are years away, but I wrote about mine hoping to put words out there to protect you, to make your girlhood and womanhood more unimpeded, unabashed, full-bodied, and empowered. I wrote "Is There Something I Should Know?" hoping to change things for you. I'm likely to have failed, but keep pushing out with your powerful self—you deserve the full world, not the diminished and restricted girl-version. Don't we all?

Brenda Shaughnessy is the author of *Our Andromeda* (one of the *New York Times'* 100 Notable Books of 2013), *Human Dark with Sugar* (James Laughlin Award and finalist for the National Book Critics Circle Award), and *Interior with Sudden Joy.* She was a Guggenheim Foundation Fellow in 2013, and is currently associate professor of English and creative writing at Rutgers University–Newark. She lives in Verona, New Jersey, with her family.

# Lannan Literary Selections

For two decades Lannan Foundation has supported the publication and distribution of exceptional literary works. Copper Canyon Press gratefully acknowledges their support.

## LANNAN LITERARY SELECTIONS 2016

Josh Bell, *Alamo Theory*

Maurice Manning, *One Man's Darkness*

Paisley Rekdal, *Imaginary Vessels*

Brenda Shaughnessy, *So Much Synth*

Ocean Vuong, *Night Sky with Exit Wounds*

## RECENT LANNAN LITERARY SELECTIONS FROM COPPER CANYON PRESS

James Arthur, *Charms Against Lightning*

Mark Bibbins, *They Don't Kill You Because They're Hungry, They Kill You Because They're Full*

Malachi Black, *Storm Toward Morning*

Marianne Boruch, *Cadaver, Speak*

Jericho Brown, *The New Testament*

Olena Kalytiak Davis, *The Poem She Didn't Write and Other Poems*

Michael Dickman, *Green Migraine*

Kerry James Evans, *Bangalore*

Tung-Hui Hu, *Greenhouses, Lighthouses*

Deborah Landau, *The Uses of the Body*

Sarah Lindsay, *Debt to the Bone-Eating Snotflower*

Lisa Olstein, *Little Stranger*

Camille Rankine, *Incorrect Merciful Impulses*

Roger Reeves, *King Me*

Richard Siken, *War of the Foxes*

Ed Skoog, *Rough Day*

Frank Stanford, *What About This: Collected Poems of Frank Stanford*

For a complete list of Lannan Literary Selections from Copper Canyon Press, please visit Partners on our website: www.coppercanyonpress.org

Poetry is vital to language and living. Since 1972, Copper Canyon Press has published extraordinary poetry from around the world to engage the imaginations and intellects of readers, writers, booksellers, librarians, teachers, students, and donors.

**WE ARE GRATEFUL FOR THE MAJOR SUPPORT PROVIDED BY:**

Anonymous
Donna and Matt Bellew
John Branch
Diana Broze
Janet and Les Cox
Beroz Ferrell & The Point, LLC
Mimi Gardner Gates
Alan Gartenhaus and Rhoady Lee
Linda Gerrard and Walter Parsons
Gull Industries, Inc.
    on behalf of William and
    Ruth True
Mark Hamilton and Suzie Rapp
Carolyn and Robert Hedin
Steven Myron Holl
Lakeside Industries, Inc.
    on behalf of Jeanne Marie Lee

Maureen Lee and Mark Busto
Brice Marden
Ellie Mathews and Carl Youngmann
    as The North Press
H. Stewart Parker
Penny and Jerry Peabody
John Phillips and Anne O'Donnell
Joseph C. Roberts
Cynthia Lovelace Sears and
    Frank Buxton
The Seattle Foundation
Kim and Jeff Seely
David and Catherine Eaton Skinner
Dan Waggoner
C.D. Wright and Forrest Gander
Charles and Barbara Wright

The dedicated interns and faithful volunteers of Copper Canyon Press

TO LEARN MORE ABOUT UNDERWRITING COPPER CANYON PRESS TITLES,
PLEASE CALL 360-385-4925 EXT. 103

The Chinese character for poetry is made up of two parts:
"word" and "temple." It also serves as pressmark for
Copper Canyon Press.

The poems are set in Minion. Headings are set in Landmark.
Printed on archival-quality paper.
Book design and composition by Phil Kovacevich.